Ee Up Lad!

A Salute to the Yorkshire Dialect

Len Markham

with illustrations by Richard Scollins

COUNTRYSIDE BOOKS
NEWBURY BERKSHIRE

First published 2002
© Len Markham and Richard Scollins 2002

COUNTRYSIDE BOOKS
3 Catherine Road
Newbury, Berkshire

To view our complete range of books,
please visit us at
www.countrysidebooks.co.uk

ISBN 1 85306 763 6

Designed by Peter Davies, Nautilus Design
Produced through MRM Associates Ltd., Reading
Typeset by Techniset Typesetters, Newton-le-Willows
Printed by J. W. Arrowsmith Ltd., Bristol

CONTENTS

FOREWORD

Like false teeth, accent, dialect and old county phrases work best in the using. For hundreds of years, each county of England had its own highly distinctive brogue and regional language. The effects of invasion, settlement, geography and climate sowed the linguistic seeds that gave us a fast disappearing oral culture that is only now being appreciated. The trend to homogenisation and the influences of our American cousins have, in just a few decades, brought what's left of our native tongue to the edge of extinction. Desist, I say, for the regional burr with its melodious words and homespun verbal wisdom that brought colour and individuality to every corner of the land is, in my view, every bit as precious as the Union Jack.

There are many academic books that soberly examine the roots of our Yorkshire language. And there is in existence a Yorkshire Dialect Society, whose sterling work keeps the old tongue alive. Long may the serious books continue to roll off the presses and God bless the enterprise of the YDS. In this book I do not pretend to compete with the more erudite studies that are available for the serious reader and researcher. Rather, from the aspect of an impressionable lad who grew up in the old West Riding and was introduced to the vernacular of the mill and mining towns at my grandad's knee, I aim to share with you the joy and fun of the old words and phrases – the guttural, the rasping, the spiky, the musical, the onomatopoeic and the highly descriptive – those gems whose continued use can spark up any conversation and keep a little part of our beloved Yorkshire alive.

Like native Yorkshire flowers, some of the ancestral words and phrases survive in isolated pockets, particularly in what remains of the old mining communities and in the more remote agricultural areas. Settled ways of life provided the social continuation and cohesion that nurtured the oral tradition bequeathed by our Anglian and Norse forebears. Passed on from generation to generation without corruption or distortion, this spoken language is the real linguistic legacy, the dialectical form of words being much older than the written rendition, that in chronological terms is comparatively new. It is no exaggeration therefore to state that the folk speech of Yorkshire is a purer form of our language than the standard English in use today and more faithful to the vernacular spoken by the people of Chaucer's day. 'Stick that in yer pipe and smoke it!' asserts the

Yorkshire farmer who decries 'boowk larning'.

In reality, it is this idiosyncratic speech that has indelibly helped to define the Yorkshireman. Every compere, actor, comedian and mimic worth his salt has the archetypal rendition of the Tyke off pat. References to flat caps, whippets and expressions such as 'There's trouble at mill', 'Ee by gum!' and 'I'm not saying my mother-in-law's ugly but every time she calls at our house, mice throw the'selves on t' traps' are in everyone's repertoire, people like the inimitable Les Dawson doing for females of the county what Compo subsequently did for the Yorkshire reputation for sartorial elegance. The TV series *Last of the Summer Wine*, centred on Holmfirth, further endorsed the somewhat fierce and volatile image of our ladies, the brush-wielding Nora Batty holding her own, in a rustic sort of way, with Britannia herself. In looking at women, Yorkshiremen, of course, pay more attention to child-bearing hips than the attractions of the mantelpiece, although they feel that the caricatures of our ladies are a tad exaggerated and insensitive. But not to worry.

We Yorkshire folk are not offended by such lampooning. Not mindful of political correctness, we have a unique capacity for laughing at ourselves. The following pages therefore take a light-hearted, self-deprecating look at the Yorkshire character, reputation and idiosyncrasies, and there are entries devoted to vocabulary and place-names. Humour infuses the pages throughout, with a score or more of illustrations by the late Richard Scollins, giving us a 'reet good laugh' and a uniquely Yorkshire insight into various exciting episodes from the history of these islands.

Len Markham
(The Wolds Ranger)

CHAPTER 1

What is a Typical Tyke?

Archetypal analyses of any distinctly different group of people are, almost without exception, misleading. Attempts at defining complex behaviour and traits usually create caricature rather than characterisation. But there are exceptions, all the nationally observed opinions of the Tyke resonating with a certain truth.

The Tyke – and in this definition I include both the male and female of the species – is predisposed to a gruff arrogance. Sitting on the backbone of England overlooking its largest county, he has every reason to entertain imperial thoughts. This Yorkshire Texas, bigger and better than any of its rivals, has produced half the nation's kings, archbishops by the sackful, explorers, scientists, industrialists, painters and poets, and more wool, coal and steel than the rest of the country combined. The Tyke's gritty self-confidence has bred a certain independence and a disdain for the effete hordes in more southerly latitudes, his stab-in-the-eye stubbornness, bluntness and brutal frankness, creating a shivering reputation on a par with that of Genghis Khan.

Such a perception would worry most folk. Not so the Tyke, who gives not a jot for any opinion but his own. One old attempt at analysing the county character exemplifies this exactly. Consider the difference between a Yorkshireman, an Irishman and a Welshman. The Welshman will not speak the truth because he cannot differentiate between the truth and a lie. The Irishman cannot speak the truth because there are always some other words that will sound better. The Yorkshireman, on the other hand, always speaks the truth because he does not give a hang for anybody on earth.

A letter written to Oliver Cromwell in 1656 by the Abbot of York would seem to endorse the above sentiment: 'There be such a company of wilful gentlemen in Yorkshire as there be not in all England besides,' he scribed. And, commenting in the 1580s, another cleric, the Archbishop of York, Edwin Sandys, endorsed this view of implacability and forthrightness, writing: 'A more stiff-necked, wilful, or obstinate people did I ever know or hear of.'

Priests and commoners alike who experienced at the sharp end the Yorkshire tenacity and thrust for a bargain, helped forge the national reputation of the

Tyke, a coat of arms coming to symbolise all his essential attributes. Reproduced opposite on a tankard, is a version of this armorial device. It consists of a horse, his beady eyes supervising a flea, a fly, a magpie and a suspended ham. Now let me explain.

The horse suggests a time-honoured inclination to buy few of the creatures, the natural propensity of our species being to steal. The flea is a reference to that particular insect's desire to bite and the stinging sensation experienced by everyone who has ever transacted any business hereabouts. The inclusion of the fly is not so much to acknowledge the Yorkshire tendency to swarm all over free food (note the Yorkshire version of grace before meals – 'God bless us all and mek us able to eyt all t'stuff 'ats on this table) but rather to honour persistence and a disposition to annoy. The inclusion of nature's most inquisitive and garrulous bird has obvious meaning, the magpie's unpretentious black and white livery also reflecting the smart but sober dress sense of your average Tyke. And so to the last icon in the quadrant, that of the hung ham – a Yorkshire joint, of course.

Mischief-makers across the border in the west – we never actually refer to the adjoining shire, lest it corrupt our children and cause overflows of swear boxes in every pub across the county – have suggested that the device refers to the need for all followers of the white rose to be strung up. This is clear calumny. The suspended ham does, of course, refer in one sense to the reality of the Tyke mellowing and maturing with age like the fabled delicacy itself. York hams have always been something to look up to and admire. Good, honest and uncomplicated; undemonstrative, invested with a love of mother earth; and in the final reckoning, sweet and rewarding, they mirror the county character precisely, even in the unsentimental masticating of the final rasher. 'He's gone 'as our Pinky. He were a good 'un, by eck he were. Did 'is job reet well. I'll miss the big fella. Bugger me! he weren't 'alf tasty.'

What other attributes are invested in the typical Tyke? Although initially wary of strangers – before we would fully trust newcomers, it was once said that we would 'summer them and winter them and summer them again' – the Yorkshireman, once he accepted an outsider, displayed rare friendship, cordiality and unshakable loyalty, bolstered by pluck, courage, endurance and a never-say-die spirit in crisis and adversity. All these qualities are symbolized by *Rosa arvensis*, the famous white rose of York, an emblem that has been flown in the thick of battle for over 500 years.

This fabled rose is celebrated in Shakespeare. In Henry VI, Richard Plantagenet says:

> *Let him that is a true-born gentleman,*
> *And stands upon the honour of his birth,*
> *If he suppose that I have pleaded truth,*
> *From off this briar pluck a white rose with me.*

No flower has been more readily identified with county pride, and legend suggests that a white rose, its petals tinged with red, still grows on those melancholy fields near York. An old ballad records that terrible battle fought between the Yorkists and the Lancastrians in a blizzard on Palm Sunday 1461:

> *Oh, the red and the white rose,*
> *On Towton Moor it grows,*
> *And red and white it blows*
> *Upon the swart for evermore;*
> *In memorial of the slaughter,*
> *When the red blood ran like water,*
> *And the victors gave no quarter*
> *In the fight on Towton Moor.*

Don't get the impression, however, that we Tykes are bloodthirsty sword-wielding thugs. We have, of course, got a surfeit of sometimes belligerent Viking chromosomes and a definite family tree that includes great uncles Eric Skullsplitter and Magnus Ripyorlegsoff. But take time to get to know us, buy us a pint – or three – and you've made an abiding friend for life.

I hope I've made the point in these few short lines that the Tyke is an exceptional fellow and is well worth the acquaintance. To readers who share the same genealogical lines, I apologize for parading the obvious, but I'm sure you'll agree that we need to convert the rest of our fellow countrymen to the notion that, such is our uniqueness, which is every bit as special as that of the Scots, we really should be the next in line for our own parliament.

To sum up, here's a ditty, written around 1850 by W.H. Burnett. With a spit-in-your-eye friendliness he rejoices in just being a native of this exceptional county:

> *Ah's Yorkshire! By my truly,*
> *Ah's, Ah's, proud ti say,*
> *Just try ya to git ower me,*
> *You'll hev eneeaf ti deea.*
>
> *Ah's open-gobbed an' soft like:*
> *Ah knaw mair than Ah tell,*
> *The fellow that wad bite me*
> *Will safe git bit hi'ssel,*
> *Ah's Yorkshire.*

CHAPTER 2

A Dictionary of Yorkshire Dialect

Following decades of unstinting earwigging in pub corners, I have gathered together my assortment of dog-eared beer mats, bus tickets and bank statements whose scribbles form the basis of this very personal lexicon of the Yorkshire language. This list of old words and phrases is as much a part of our Yorkshire heritage as our famous pudding. So the next time you're in the snug try it out!

Ackers	Money; compare *brass*.
Acting the goat	Behaving stupidly.
Addled	Bad, rotten, drunk.
Afire	On fire; 'the chimney's gone afire': an old whaling term signifying that the whale is spouting blood.
Agate	To start, get on with.
Ah'll give thi what for!	
	'I'll chastise you or give you a good thumping.'
Airt	A point or part of the horizon or compass.
Alicker	Vinegar.
An all	Also.
Apiece	Each.
Appen	Perhaps.
A time er two	Understated frequency; 'I've heard that a time er two'.
Arran	A spider or spider's web.
Arse about face	Completely the wrong way round.
Arse 'oled	Extremely well intoxicated; compare *rat arsed*.
Article	A person; a mildly derogatory personal term.
Arvill	A funeral.
As fit as a lop	As fit as a flea.

As queer as Dick's at-band
Sullen, morose and taciturn.

As lazy as Ludlam's dog
The dog in question guarded the wine bins of Ludlam, who kept an alehouse in Scotland Street, Sheffield, about 1787; it was so idle that it laid its head against the wall to bark.

As soft as a boiled tonnap
Lacking mental ability.

As snug as a bug in a rug
Warm and cosy (especially in a warm bed or thick clothing).

Aske	A newt.
Auturs	Strange.
Av got all on	Fully committed with no spare time.
Babber-pants	Cowardly.

Back'ards and for'ards
Intimacy between a man and a woman.

Back-endish	Autumnal.
Backslaver	An impudent and cheeky verbal response.
Backword	Cancellation or postponement.
Badly	Poorly; feeling unwell.
Band	String.
Bar	Without; complete.
Barmpot	An extremely silly fellow.
Barn or ba'an	A child.
Beeal	To cry out, to weep.
Beer off	Off-licence.
Beeskep	Beehive.
Belt	To pummel, to hit hard; to chastise (especially with a belt).
Beltenger	A hard blow.
Belter	Exceptional, nonpareil.
Besom	An immoral woman.
Betwaddled	Confused (brought on by intoxication).
Bewk-larning	Formal education.

A DICTIONARY OF YORKSHIRE DIALECT

Bink	A bench.
Black-bright	Extremely mucky.
Blackclock	The black beetle.
Blendings	Peas and beans mixed together.
Bletherskite	Trivial conversation.
Blowed	Nonplussed, dumbfounded, overwhelmed.
Bobby-dazzler	An excitingly dressed person.
Bogie	A children's cart made from surplus wood and reclaimed pram wheels.
Booke and bane	Lusty and strong.
Boon	Ready.
Boorly	Gross or overly large.
Bottery	The elder tree.
Bowken	To choke on something; to retch.
Brahma	An excellent or superior example of its type. (The term may have been introduced by ex-Indian Army soldiers, deriving from the Hindu deity. Alternatively it may have its source in the introduction in 1778 of the water closet by Yorkshire inventor and engineer Joseph Bramah.)
Brass	Money.
Braying	Hitting; knocking the living daylights out of; to assaulting someone with the fists.

Brimstone and treacle

An old home remedy for boils, consisting of a mixture of flowers of sulphur and black treacle. Administered by several bare armed women who held the victim down, prised open the mouth and thrust successive ladlesfull of the magma down the gullet, the remedy was as effective at removing boils as Vesuvius was at wiping out all life in Pompeii. But beware the vented fumes and aftershocks.

Browned off	Fed up with life, disgruntled; feeling sorry for oneself.
Brussen	Boastful; having a lot of; bursting (as in over eating).
Bugger	A mild and a hugely expressive expletive widely used by both adults and children (in Yorkshire, the word has no sexual connotations); a mischievous, often likeable rogue.

Bugger it! An exclamation of frustration meaning 'I've had enough of this!'

Bummlekites Blackberries.

Cagmag Poor quality gristly meat.

Caingel A toothy, crabbed fellow.

Cake 'oil The mouth.

Call To criticize.

Canny Careful: shrewd.

Capped Astonished, surprised.

Cat's cock hair Miniscule amount.

Cauf-licked Afflicted by consistently unruly hair.

Cazzons Dried cattle dung.

Champion Exceptionally good; in fine fettle.

Char To chide.

Charver Friend, old mate.

Chelp To sound off; to answer back.

Chip 'oil A fish and chip emporium.

Chuff To pontificate; to have a lot of; a rear end 'I couldn't give a monkey's chuff'.

Chumpin To gather together timber for the November 5th bonfire.

Clap cold Stone cold, especially of food.

Clarty Besmirched with dirt; muddy.

Chunter Babbling complaint.

Clapperclaw To beat with the open hand.

Cleg Horsefly.

Clout To smack with the hand.

Clouts Over garment or knickers.

Coarser A kerb; footpath edge.

Coggers Compressed snow and ice adhering to footwear.

Cool the haggas To beat soundly.

Cowclap A cow-pat. Summer warmth bakes these bovine cruds, whose crusts, like frozen winter puddles, are irresistible to young boys with sticks.

A DICTIONARY OF YORKSHIRE DIALECT

Cronk	To huddle or crouch, especially for warmth.
Crambazzled	Prematurely aged as a consequence of a hedonistic lifestyle.
Cruse	Pleased.
Cussen	Dark, gloomy, overcast.
Cussen-muck	Piles of spoil left by quarrying operations.
Cutter	Soft, gentle, lilting talk.
Dateless	Stupid, not having a clue.
Degg-bound	Mightily swelled in the belly.
Dindle	To experience a tingling, tremulous sensation after a blow.
Doit	To lapse into a state of forgetfulness and confusion brought on by old age.
Ding	To strike.
Dip	Liquified frying fat, usually lard or beef dripping, especially when poured over a cooked breakfast to make it even more appetising.
Don't gerrim going	
	Plea to desist from provocative statements in the interests of not arousing the predictable anger and annoyance of a third party.
Dowled	Flat (of liquor).
Doylem	A stupid fellow.
Dowly	Grim; low-spirited.
Dozand leauke	An old withered look.
Drop o' York	The scaffold on the Knavesmire.
Druft	A drying breeze, a thirst.
Duffy	Overly dry and light.
Durdam	Commotion.

Ee by gum lad	Breezy greeting implying that by any comparative measure of the day's pleasures, 'it's good to see thi.'

Ee up lad!   General cheery salutation.

Ee'd eat oven door if it were buttered.
     'He's prodigiously greedy.'

Ee's as fine as a fart wi' a frill on.
     'That dandy is a little overdressed.'

Ee's that tight ee won't let his teeth chatter when ee freezes.
     'He taught Scrooge how to peel an orange in his pocket.'

Ey up!   'See here! Look out!' 'How are you?'

Faantickles   Face freckles.

Fain   Glad, very pleased.

Fair rosined   Replete and rosy with ale.

Far end   The opposite side.

Fastening penny   A symbolic payment to signify an informal agreement between an employer and his hired hand.

Fetch   To bring, to carry along.

Fettle   To give a good seeing to, often in a sexual context

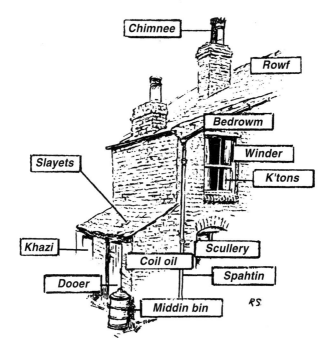

A DICTIONARY OF YORKSHIRE DIALECT

Fezzon on	To seize fiercely.
Fixfax	The sinews of the neck of cattle.
Flacker	To tremble.
Flig	Able to fly.
Flitterkins	An expression of concern and surprise.
Flit	To move house.
Flummoxed	Bamboozled, at a loss.
Flustered	Confused, at sixes and sevens.
Foggie	To go first in children's games.
Foisty	Musty; turning rancid.
Fra	From.
Frag	To fill up.
Frame thissen!	'Get organised!'
Fratch	To argue.
Frem	Strange.
Frit	Scared or frightened.
Frozz	Frozen.
Frumenty	A type of sweetened, spiced porridge eaten at Christmas.
Fuddle	An entertainment; a party usually accompanied by food and drink.
Fufflement	Extravagant and over elaborate clothing.
Full up	Replete, satiated.
Gab	To chatter idly.
Gammerstangs	A great, foolish, wanton girl.
Gang	An adit or gallery in a lead mine.
Gansey	A traditional hand-knitted fisherman's pullover. (Individual styles and stitch types identify individual communities and even separate fishing families.)
Garth	Yard.
Gas tar	Bitumen that in hot weather expanded and oozed between the street cobbles. (Collected by youngsters and rolled into balls, it made extremely sticky and smelly *taws*, whose staining qualities on cuffs and collars defied even Persil.)

Gate	Road or way.
Gawpead	Daft person.
Gawve	To stare.
Get shut on	To relieve yourself of a possession (said, for example, when the TV detector van is spied turning down the street).
Ginnel	A narrow passage between buildings (see *snicket*).
Give ower!	'Stop it!'
Gliffe	A sudden chance sighting.
Glimps, also **glimes**	Cunning looks.
Glorfat	Extremely fat.
Gimmer	A female lamb.
Gizzen	To cry.
Gob	The mouth.
Gobby	Predisposed to exaggerated and conceited talk.
Gormless	Lacking in mental ability; eleven pence to the bob.
Got the monk on	Sulky.
Gowk	The cuckoo.
Gradley	Fine or excellent.
Graith	Riches.
Greck	The runt of the litter; a derisory term for a person who is odd and eccentric.
Guytresh	An imp or evil spirit.
Hallocked	Teased, bullied; worried.
Handclout	A towel.
Hand of glory	A gory good luck charm used by burglars. It was said to miraculously open locks and send the unfortunate inhabitants of the burgled house to sleep. But first catch your hand! It had to be ritualistically hacked from an executed criminal, embalmed, dried in the sun and fitted with a candle made from human fat and tallow. Its flame could only be extinguished by dousing with skimmed milk or blood!
Happen	Maybe, perhaps.
Har	A thick and persistent fog. Compare *roke*.
Hard on	Fast asleep.

A DICTIONARY OF YORKSHIRE DIALECT

Hardlins Hardly.

Heart sluffened Emotionally grieved.

Hells bells and buckets o' blood
An exclamation of surprise and pained astonishment.

He'll stand fer coal on 'is 'ead
Remark alluding to gullibility and a capacity for being taken advantage of.

Helm A shed.

Hensilver Money distributed by a bridegroom to the men of the village, who would retire to the village inn to celebrate and sing a traditional song:

Oh, here's a good health to the bride of yond house
That's provided us all this good cheer;
Lord send her health,
Lord prosper her wealth,
And may we be married next year.
It's fair to be seen he's drunk it off clean
As any other man can,
And if that he please
Another at his ease
And it should be unto a good man.

He's plenty o' blood but no suet
'He comes from a distinguished aristocratic line but he's potless.'

Hig A short, sharp, passing burst of bad weather. **Takes the hig** show temporary displeasure or sulkiness at some conduct or remark which is disapproved off.

Hockey The last load of harvest.

Hook A rogue or a shady character.

Hotter To shake.

Hubbleshoo Loud babbling; commotion; noisy assemblage.

Hug To carry.

I ampt gorrit on me.
'Sorry, I can't pay you today.'

Idle back A rod rest.

If his brains were dynamite, they wouldn't blow his cap off.
> 'In comparison with Hercule Poirot's "little grey cells", that chap's been short changed.'

If the wind changes, tha'll stay like that.
> A mocking rebuke meaning: If the wind changes direction, it will cause the contorted face of the person so addressed to remain in a permanent state of grimace.

I haven't two ha'pennies for a penny.
> An oft repeated phrase when purses become empty meaning: 'I'm skint'.

I'll go to our 'ouse!; I'll go t' foot o' our stairs! or, I'll stand the drop o' York!
> Expressions of surprise and astonishment.

Ill-thriven   Malnourished or thin.

I'm bustin' fer a slash.
> 'I'm rather in need of the netty.'

Intake   Land reclaimed to agriculture from rough moorland.

It'd pay thi'   'There'd be a benefit (not necessarily financial) in following my recommendations.'

It's an overcoat colder.
> 'It's turned decidedly more chilly.'

It's a tale.   'It's not a very plausible story' (said with some humour, but with no suggestion that the tale-teller is lying).

It's gerrin' a bit black ower our Bill's mother's.
> 'The dark clouds over there portend heavy rain.'

It's sighlin dahn!   'It's raining very heavily.'

Jart   To hit.

Jaup   To make a noise like liquor agitated in a closed vessel.

Jauping up   Beating, whisking.

Jay-legged   Knock-kneed.

Jeremy Joy   The thrush.

A DICTIONARY OF YORKSHIRE DIALECT

Jibber   A horse or a person easily discouraged by difficulties or adversity.

Jiggered   Tired out; exhausted.

Jinny-Hoog-Me-Claus
   Cleavers (the pernicious weed).

Jock   Sandwiches, food, lunch.

Jokashus   Full of fun; humorous.

Joskin   A country worker.

Jubberty   An obstacle or misfortune.

Judycow   The ladybird.

Jumble   Traditional gingerbread cake dusted in sugar.

Juntersome   Cantankerous, ill-tempered; morose.

Just noo   At once; in a moment.

K'tons   Curtains.

Kall   To gossip without purpose (an exclusively female occupation).

Kecks   Trousers or underpants.

Kelter   To state.

Kenspeckle   Easily recognisable; easy to be seen.

Ket   Rubbish.

Kick-out-can   A children's game – an empty can is left in a circle drawn on the ground, the 'it' person having to seek out his fellows before they can beat him to kicking the can 'out'.

Kincough   Whooping cough.

Kist   A large storage trunk or box.

Kizzened   Withered, wizened.

Knobble   To hit with a stick.

Knur and spell   An adult game whose object is to hit a ball (the knur) the furthest distance with a clubbed stick (the *pummel*). The knur is ejected from a hurling machine (the spell) by depressing a sprung trigger.

Kye   Cows.

Kysty   Hard to please, quick to pick fault.

Lafter   All the eggs laid by a hen between two separate broodings.

Laggie	The last participant to take a turn in a children's game (see also foggie and seggie).
Laiking	Playing; taking part, usually in games or sport.
Lame under t'cap	A little slow on the up-take.
Land	To deploy a chastising hand in punishment.
Lant	Urine.
Lant hole	A channelled aperture in the external wall of a building through which urine was poured; urine was collected daily for use in the textile industry.
Lap	To devour greedily, especially of drink; to enwrap in clothing.
Laverock	The skylark.
Layer-father	An instructor, teacher or prompter.
Leap	A large, deep wicker basket.
Leet on	To come across unexpectedly.
Let's be reet	'Let us talk truthfully.'
Like 'oss muck, he's allus in t'road.	
	'He's perennially in the way.'
Ligged	Lying down.
Lip	Insolent verbal rejoinder or comment (often attributed to youngsters who respond to adult criticism).
Loiner	A native of Leeds.
Loosing	Coming to an end or leaving (of cinema or theatre performances).
Lollicker	The tongue.
Lolling	Slouching.
Lop	A flea (long included in the Yorkshire coat of arms).
Lop	Fisherman's term for an ocean chop or swell.
Love	Friendly, old-fashioned form of address (directed at both males and females).
Lowance	A midday break from agricultural work, traditionally marked by the provision of free food and drink supplied by the farmer's wife.
Lownd	Calm (of the sea).

A DICTIONARY OF YORKSHIRE DIALECT

Lowped   Jumped, leaped.

Lungeous   Dangerous; aggressive.

Lunt   Light; flame.

Lurgy   An unspecified disease. The word is shouted when a child is touched during the game of tig conferring a pestilence that can only be got rid of by a similar passing on.

Lyke wake   The ceremonial surrounding the disposal of the dead, particularly on the North York Moors. The Lyke Wake Walk from Osmotherley to Ravenscar takes its name from the ancient rituals, passing over routes on the moors where coffins were taken for burial.

Maddle   To fluster or confuse.

Maiden   A clothes-horse; see also *winter edge*.

Main   Very.

Mainswear   To swear falsely.

Maister   Master; a person in charge or in authority.

Mardy   Broody, sulky; spoilt.

Mardy-arse   Sour and mean spirited person.

Marrer   Close friend and compatriot.

Mash   To make tea.

Maungy   Ill-tempered, awkward and uncooperative.

Maunsell   An unkempt and unattractive woman.

Mawgram   A facial grimace as indicating distaste or unease.

Mawk   A complaining, persistently whining, woe is me person – especially a woman.

Meg   A halfpenny – I haven't a meg. 'I am in a state of total penury.'

Mell Supper Traditional feast celebrating the gathering in of the harvest. The menu included sirloin of beef, legs of mutton, rabbit and chicken pies, plum pudding and brandy sauce, cheese and nut brown ale.

Mend   To repair or replenish, as in mending or adding more fuel to the fire.

Menseful   Clean; thrifty.

Middin	A refuse or dung heap; the term is used derogatively to describe household conditions.
Middlin	About average; neither good nor bad; in between.
Mind!	'Take heed of what I say.'
Mint	To faint.
Mipe	To move silently and furtively.
Mischief Neet	November 4th. Always an important day in the calendar of small boys, it gives any mischievous urchin immunity from arrest for such crimes as knocking on doors and running away, smearing door knobs with treacle and pushing fire crackers through letter boxes – done in memory of fellow Yorkshireman, Guy Fawkes.
Missen	Myself.
Mizzle	Very fine *roke*, combined with drizzle.
Modther	Murder.
Moodiewarp	The mole.
Moot out	Deterioration of old clothes characterised by gradually developing tears and holes.
Moss	Bog or low marshy ground.
Mother Shipton	Famous soothsayer who, it is claimed, predicted the end of Wolsey, the coming of the Armada, the outbreak of the English Civil War and the advent of the railways. Her name is forever associated with the town of Knaresborough and her cave and wishing well near the River Nidd.
Moy	Muggy.
Mud	Might.
Muff	A hardly discernible sound.
Mullock	A mess, disarray; a confused and badly organized outcome.
Mun	Must.
Munk	Pique; a sulking demeanour. 'He's got a reet munk on.'
Nack	A round shallow depression scooped out of the ground for the game of *taws*.
Napper	The head.
Naught cottens weel.	
	'Nothing goes right.'

A DICTIONARY OF YORKSHIRE DIALECT

Neeaf	A fist.
Near	Parsimonious, tight with money.
Neb	The peak of a cap; a nose, a beak.
Nesh	Physically weak or soft; unable to cope with the normal rigours of life.
Netty	A privy, a toilet.
New cake	A usually round loaf of bread, traditionally baked in a Yorkshire range oven.
Nicely	In good physical or financial condition.
Nip-curn	A parsimonious or miserly person.
Nithered:	Perishing cold.
Nobble	Mischievous, misleading talk; humorous banter.
Nobbut	Only.
Noration	A hullabaloo, a loud commotion.
Oft cummed en	A newcomer to the district; an outsider.
Oil	A hole or place; hence **chip oil**, **coal oil**, **cake oil** (mouth) **lug oil** (ear).
On Ilkla Moor baht 'at	
	'On Ilkley Moor without a hat' (part of the famous Yorkshire anthem).
Orts	Leftovers, scraps, fragmentary remains.
Over-faced	Presented with too much to eat.
Over many	An unappreciated abundance.
Owmer	Shade.
Owt	Anything.
Owt like?	'Anything like?' – an enquiry as to whether the object of the conversation is up to standard.
Oxter	The armpit.
Paddle	To slide or move erratically especially in muddy conditions.
Pancrack	The dole or unemployment benefit: 'He's on the pancrack.'
Pap	Teat.
Parkin	A cake made from oatmeal, ginger and treacle, traditionally eaten on Bonfire Night.

Parzel	To walk slowly.
Patty	A fried fishcake, traditionally made from fish sandwiched between slices of potato (particularly common in Hull and the East Riding, where, in the interests of price, herbs are sometimes substituted for fish).
Peeart	Lively, fit, brisk.
Penk	To inspect sneakily and closely with the eyes.
Pen wark	Letter writing; keeping accounts.
Piece	A length of cloth.
Pig cheer	The local distribution of pig offal to needy villagers.
Piggy	A children's game – a version of *knur and spell*. The piggy is a short, fat peg, sharpened to a point a both ends, which is hit with a stick on one end as it lies on the ground; it is then hit again in the air, the winner of the game being the one who knocks it the furthest distance.
Piggy-jack	Nursery name for the pig; see also *bah lamb* and *tushy peg*.
Pike	A sty or pustule.
Pikelet	A Yorkshire name for the toasted crumpet.
Pine	To crave sustenance.
Plothery	Muddy.
Pluff	To blow at anything.
Pluther	Liquid manure; sludge.
Pobs	Softened food made easily digestible for children, invalids and old people.
Pogged	Full up, replete with food.
Polesmitten	Mad; crazy.
Popped up	Full of ale, drunk.
Potless	Having no money.
Pots	The washing up.
Powlin'	Ultra short haircut.
Pubble	(Of corn and women) plump, full bodied.
Puddled	Dim witted.
Pummel	A stick with a clubbed end; see *knur and spell*.

A DICTIONARY OF YORKSHIRE DiALECT

Put wood in't 'ole!

'Would you kindly shut the door.'

Quarrel   A flagstone; a glass pane.

Queer stick   Someone who acts in an odd or bizarre fashion.

Quicks   A hawthorn sapling used for hedge making.

Rack o' t'ee   The calculation and adjustment of measurements and proportions by line of sight; phrase is used by craftsman in trades such as stone masonry and carpentry. Although tools such as rulers and gauges are dispensed with, this technique can be incredibly accurate when performed by skilled practitioners.

Raggald   A criminal or ruffian.

Rasselled   Withered like an apple.

Rat arsed   Falling over as a consequence of over indulgence in strong liquor; compare arse 'oled.

Reckon   To consider; to evaluate, to weigh up.

Relievio   A children's chase and catch game. After a pursuit, one child physically apprehends another with the words, 'Two, four, six, eight, ten, collared caught!' Afterwards, this 'prisoner' is taken to a den where he has to remain until he is touched and 'relieved' by the other marauding children, who themselves risk capture. The game is over when all the children are incarcerated.

Renky   Tall and athletic.

Rick   To give off fumes.

Rifting   Belching; farting.

Rigweltered: (Of beasts) up-ended, on the back with the feet in the air. The term has given its name to a popular strong beer brewed in the famous Yorkshire brewing town of Masham.

Rive To move about with little purpose; to tear at something; to snatch.

Rive all a-dawds To tear everything to pieces.

Road Way or method. 'Yer going aboot it wrong road.'

Roaring Profusely weeping.

Roil To romp joyously, as of young children.

Roke A dense, rolling sea-fog that often spreads far inland.

Roven Torn.

Routering time Spring-cleaning time.

Ruttle The guttural sound emanating from the nasal passages and airways as a result of coughing and mucus clearing.

Saim Cooking fat or lard.

Sam To garner; to collect up.

Sandwich A popular ice-cream confection served between two sweet biscuits by itinerant salesmen.

Sark A shirt.

Scarborough warning An early, usually verbal and confidential indication of brewing trouble – associated with an historic assault on the famous seaside castle.

Scarborough woof An east coast name for the dogfish.

Scaur A jutting ledge at the foot of a cliff.

Scrag To pull about and dishevel a fellow pupil in the school playground.

Scollops Fried thickly sliced potatoes.

Scraffle To crawl in haste.

Scran Any foodstuff; the process of eating (not daintily).

Scrat To scratch persistently and offensively; to make a poor and a precarious living.

Scug To hide.

Seg A metal stud with a sharp point for hammering into the soles of shoes to minimize wear. These were once produced by the million in Leeds.

Seggie   The second participant to take a turn in a children's game; see also *foggie* and *laggie*.

She's as straight up and down as a yard o' pump watter.
'If that woman needed a bra, there'd be enough material in a finger poke.'

She's wedded the midden for the sake of the muck.
'She's married a disreputable fellow for his money.'

Shift thissen, lad! 'Kindly remove your body (in its comatose state it's an insult to the concept of work and an impediment to proper locomotion).'

Shoe-cross   An archaic good luck charm whereby crossing a shoe with a licked finger was thought to bring good fortune.

Shold   Slipper.

Shop   An indeterminate location or place; hence, all over the shop.

Sick way   The anti-clockwise movement of a playground roundabout, said by children to induce vomiting.

Sickened off   Repelled by some distasteful act or occurrence.

Sided by   Buried (referring to a funeral).

Sikan   Such.

Siling   Pouring down with rain.

Sind   To rinse or wash out.

Sithee   'See you', an introductory verbal thrust across the bows inviting the listener to hear some real Yorkshire wisdom.

Skeal   School.

Skeg   To look; to glance or peep.

Skeller   To squint.

Skel up   To overturn.

Skep   A basket.

Skitters   Diarrhoea.

Slack   Hollow.

Slaape   Slippery.

Slaver   Impudent backchat or criticism.

Sluffened	Depressed, disheartened; browned off.
Smittled	Cross-infected with an infectious disease or illness.
Smoot	A gap at the base of a dry stone wall allowing access between fields by sheep.
Snap	Midday packed lunch (peculiar to the West Riding; in the East Riding workers had their *lowances*.
Snawke	To smell.
Sneck	Door latch.
Snicket	A narrow alleyway, particularly in the old West Riding.
Snickleway	A narrow passageway, especially in York.
Snizy	Bitterly cold.
Snurles	The nostrils.
Sowl	To pull about in water.
Spang the gates	To make haste.
Spanish	A stick of liquorice confectionary.
Spatterdashers	Coverlets worn above the stockings to protect from 'mire and dirt'.
Spell	A splinter of wood in the flesh (usually prized out with a sharp needle).
Spice	Any type of confectionary.
Spice cake	A rich fruit cake, traditionally baked for Christmas.
Stingo	A strong, north-country ale.
Splutterment	Abuse or backchat.
Sprag	To tell tales.
Sprog	To spit.
Spuggy	A sparrow.
Staith	Seaside landing stage or quay.
Stalled	Bored and totally uninterested.
Stee	A ladder.
Stick out like chapel 'at pegs	To be prominent, not easily missed or lost sight of.
Stife	Strong tasting.
Stoupe	An erect stone or gatepost.

CHAPTER 3

A local Skeg at Nursery Rhymes

Wackford Squeers, the Yorkshire schoolmaster in Charles Dickens' novel *Nicholas Nickleby*, used dialect words and phrases like these, and, like most Tykes, he had a brusque and practical bent:

'This is the first class in English spelling and philosophy, Nickleby', said Squeers, beckoning Nicholas to stand behind him... now then, where's the first boy?'

'Please, Sir, he's cleaning the back parlour window,' said the temporary head of the philosophical class.

'So he is, to be sure,' rejoined Squeers. 'We go upon a practical mode of teaching, Nickleby; the regular education system. C-l-e-a-n, clean, verb active, to make bright, to scour. W-i-n, win, d-e-r, der, winder, a casement. When the boy knows this out of book, he goes and does it.'

To take a leaf out of the imposing Mr Squeers' book, now you've had a good look at the above lists, have a go at this:

'Yah daay yan o' them girt beears gat hissen sadly tenged wi' a bee. He wer seea despe'tly ho'tten was t'beear at he wer wahld ommeeast. Noo, they're a varry lungeous thing is a beear, an seea ti mak 'em think on t'next tahm, he maks nowt ti deea bud he off ti t'gardin an' clicks t' beeskep ower wi sikan a bat. Noo, by that, mun, ther was a bonny ti-deea; t'bees was sairly putten aboot, an' seea they all com a' beear, an' leeted on him; an' he were tenged all ower, whahl it leeaked agin they wer boun to rahve him i'bits; an' he wer hard set to ger away frev 'em wick.

'Varry seean he was swidgin' an' warkin' awhahl he could hardlins bahd; bud, hooivver, he set hissen doon upo' t'grund ti beeal, an' he shakk'd his head an' scatted his lugs an' sike leyke. Eftther he'd gotten settled doon a bit, thinks he tiv hissen, ah mebbe mud as weel ae tae'n neea noatis eftther t'fo'st bee tanged ma, as ti a'e meead sikan a durdam amang t'others, awhahl they were fit ti modther ma; an' it wer all ti neea use a t'finish.'

Understand it? Well, if you're having a little difficulty, here's a translation:

'A bear happened to be stung by a bee, and the pain was so acute that in the madness of revenge he ran into the garden and overturned the hive. This outrage provoked their anger to a high degree, and brought the fury of the whole swarm upon him. They attacked him with such violence that his life was in danger, and it was with the utmost difficulty that he made his escape wounded from head to tail. In this desperate condition, lamenting his misfortunes and licking his sores, he could not forbear reflecting how much more advisable it had been to have acquiesced patiently under one injury than thus by an unprofitable resentment to have provoked a thousand.'

And here for good measure is another short comprehension test. It's a verbatim copy of a letter written in 1825.

> Dear Mudder and Fadder
>
> Ah left me plase last mundey murnin me master and I differed about levng foad yat open, now fadder dunnet be vext at ma for telling you truth at mater now you se I ad to gan doun to osmaley te get pleaf airen shaped and wile I was stannin ower fire it com in te me hede that I had left foad yat open and wen I went back agan he sware that he wad kick me and ast him wat for and sed that sue had gitten in anondert emmel and eten hoalt gease eags but has gannen to stop at me unkle willes twea thre days then I sal come yam an tel ye all aboute it.
>
> Ahs stil your lovle Sun
>
> dickey

What was Dickey's misdemeanour? He left the gate open!

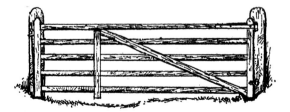

A Local Skeg at Nursery Rhymes

The Grand Old Duke of York

CHAPTER 4

The Yorkshire Mining Tradition

Mining for lead and coal has been carried on in Yorkshire for centuries, the first tentative exploitations of both commodities tapping into surface veins and outcroppings. Go to the Dales today and you will observe rashes of greened-over bell pits and a vast abandoned legacy of spoil heaps, blocked-up tunnels, levels and ruined ore crushing and smelting buildings. Paradoxically, these landscape-scaring memories of the lead mining industry

THE COLLIER'S CHANGING IMAGE

1. c.1877

2 c.1900

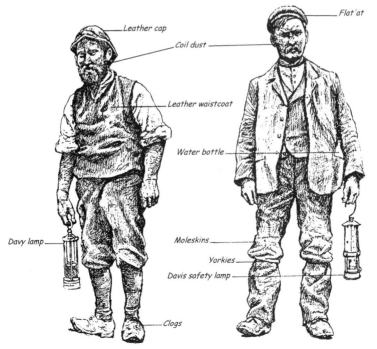

Leather cap

Coil dust

Flat 'at

Leather waistcoat

Water bottle

Davy lamp

Moleskins

Yorkies

Davis safety lamp

Clogs

outlive many of the more recent visual eyesores created by coal mining. In a drive to modernity and regeneration, much of the despoliation and disfigurement associated with the Yorkshire coalfield has been swept away and ameliorated in recent years, scores of pits and thousands of miners having been made redundant. However, the proud mining traditions and folklore of a mighty enterprise that once employed over a quarter of a million men live on in the many local words and expressions and a mischievous sense of humour that the harsh conditions and specialist nature of the industry produced.

The drawings on these pages show the changing attire and equipment of local coalminers down the decades, leather caps, breeches and clogs giving way to safety helmets, boiler suits and steel-reinforced boots in the latter years of the industry. In the early days, candles and simple lamps were the only form of illumination available. Then came the Wolf Safety Lamp. It originated in

THE COLLIER'S CHANGING IMAGE

3. *c.1930*

4. *c.1977*

Glass-fibre safety helmet

Battery lamp

Flat 'at

Coil dust

Boiler suit

Canteen

Self-rescuer

Snap-tin

Wolf safety lamp

Knee-pads

Garforth type 6 flame safety lamp

THE YORKSHIRE MINING TRADITION

Germany during the 1890s, but was replaced by an improved pattern manufactured in Leeds from 1905 until the outbreak of the Second World War. Note also the ubiquitous snap tin. 'Snap', in coal mining parlance, is a packed lunch, although the word infiltrated every level of society in the old West Riding.

The drawings, however, do not tell the whole story of mining fashion. Plunging into the bowels of the earth was hot work and sometimes male miners dispensed with clothing altogether, their female counterparts on occasion following their lead. The following is an extract from a commissioners' report on mining in the West Riding coalfield in the 1840s:

> In many of the collieries there is no distinction of sex. The labour is distributed indifferently among both sexes, excepting that it is comparatively rare for the women to hew or get the coals, although there are numerous instances in which they regularly perform even this work. In great numbers of coal pits in this district the men work in a state of perfect nakedness, and in this state are assisted in their labour by females of all ages, from girls of six years old to women of twenty one, these females being themselves quite naked down to the waist.

Second only to deep-sea fishing in terms of accidents and fatalities, mining has always been a tough and dangerous occupation. But with typical Yorkshire phlegm, the miners always made light of their occupation:

> 'Some blokes went faint at the sight of a shovel. I've seen more work in an Asprin.'

> 'This particlar miner were a bit of a lad. Afore they opened pithead baths he'd get washed in front o' t'fire like everyone else. Anyhow, he had a fancy women he'd call on, on his way 'ome. It were a bit o' a mystery though, him alus ending up wi' a clean 'bit' and his missis eventually smelled a rat. "How come," she says "that every part o' yer body is mucky except that 'bit'." "Well, I'll tell thee, you stupid woman," he answers as quick as a flash. "I stopped by at the khazi on me way 'ome and had a swill there." Once bitten twice shy as they say. Well, after that he'd take his dusty cap and blacken hissen up afore he got home.'

CHAPTER 5

Old Yorkshire Sayings, Banter and Wisdom

It'll save tha' no small trouble,
If when speeaking you tek care,
Of whom you speeak, to whom you speeak,
And hoo, and when and where.

Noo John I knaws tha hasn't much moor time in this 'ere life. Tha's deeing tis certain. But tha mun hang on a bit longer like. Tha knaws it's a longish steeap to t'churchyard and tharn be a bonny weight. Likely ahl be yan o' yer bearers so hang on a bit longer. I can see tha's lost a bit o' flesh, but tha's nowt like been bedfast for tekkin flesh off; na hang on a bit longer.

Here's tiv us all on us! me an' all.
May we nivver want nowt, noan on us.
Nor me nawther!

It's a poor belly 'at can't warm a drop of ale.

It's mebbe nut very genteel ti pick bones wi' yer teeth, but gentry losses a lot o' sweet meeat wi' their fine manners. Nearer t'bone sweeter t'meeat.

OLD YORKSHIRE SAYINGS, BANTER & WISDOM

What is it has fower stiff standers, fower dilly danders, two lookers, two crookers and a wig wag? (Why, it's a cow of course!)

Never cast a clout 'til May is out.

Yain, tain, eddero, peddero, pitts, tayter, later, overro, coverro, dix, yain-dix, tain-dix, eddero-dix, peddero-dix, bumfit, yain-o-bumfit, tain-o-bumfit, edder-bumfit, peddero-bumfit, jiggit. (Words of a Yorkshire shepherd counting his sheep.)

Some lads' bellies is like bottomless pits, and others has eyes bigger than their bellies – they'll eat till they're brussen and rifting.

I say nowt to nobody about nowt in no road, for, says I, least said soonest mended, and then nothin' can be twisted, and badness putten to it in noway whatsumdever.

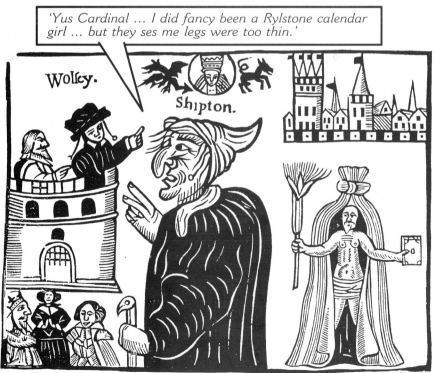

47

Mair rain, mair rest;
Fine weather's not allus best.

There's allus most thrusting weer there's least room.

Never put thee husband on t'pedestal – eel nobbut want dusting.

Here lies she who seldom ly'd
Whose skills often has been try'd
Her Prophecies shall still survive
And ever keep her name alive.

Epitaph to Mother Shipton

It's a good horse that never stumbles and a good wife that never grumbles.

Good luck gives to some more than they ought to have, but seldom more than they want.

Some say that those of us who live all our days here don't appreciate it. I must be different. I do. I know I could be happy nowhere else. I know, because I once tried it. How fain I was to get

back here. There's nothing like it.

(A Yorkshire farmer writing in the 1940s)

Our dead brother was yan of them what didn't wait to be asked when he knew somebody was fast for a man, a hoss and cart, or a bit o' ready money. He was a good nybor, and if he couldn't say nowt good about anybody, he said nowt at all. He was a chap what had a kind smile and word for everybody. He allus believed the best of folks and, although he was often taken in, he trusted folks. Nobody liked a droll tale better than him; nobody laughed more through his life, but he couldn't bide mucky stories, or a lot of lowse talk and swearing. If company he was in began anything of that there he used to get up and say: 'When you begins with those vulgar fractions, it's no spot for me, so I'll bid you all good day!' Folks respected him for it, for everybody who knew him knew he wasn't a killjoy. He used ti say: 'I like folks and horses what has quality, good action, sound and honest eyes and no vice.' If he hasn't gone to heaven, a lot on us has a poor chance o' landing there'.

A neighbourly tribute to a Yorkshire farmer
given at his funeral in the 1920s, quoted in
Yorkshire Village Life, Humour and Characters
by J. Fairfax – Blakeborough

CHAPTER 6

Yorkshire Song Book

Yorkshire has a long tradition of song writing, much of the county character finding its way into age-old lyrics ... so strike up the piano!

THE VIRGIN RACE or York-shire's Glory

Being an account of a Race lately run at Temple-Newsham-Green; none being admitted to run but such as were Virgins. (Tune is a 'New Game at Cards')

You that do desire to hear
Of a virgin race run in York-shire,
Come and listen, I'll declare,
Such news before you ne'r did hear;
For, I think, since the world begun,
But seldom virgins races run.

Four virgins that supposed were
A race did run, I now declare:
Sure such a race was never seen,
As this at Temple Newsham Green;
In half shirts and drawers these maids did
*   run,*
But Bonny Nan the race has won.

A silver spoon this Nan obtain'd;
The next a silver bodkin gain'd;
The third that was not so quite as nimble,
Was to have a silver thimble;
And she that was the last of all,
Nothing unto her share did fall.

In drawers red Ann Clayton run,
And she it was the race that won;
Pegg Hall, as I may tell you,
Did run in drawers that were blew;
Honest Alice Hall that was third,
Here drawers were white upon my word.

A concourse great of people were,
For to behold these virgins there,
Who so well acted the man's part,
And love a man with all their heart;
But what means this for well we know
Maids through the nation all do so.

Now let us come to Bonny Nan,
Who won a race once of a man;
In Bassing-hall street he did dwell,
His name was Luke, 'tis known full well;
And let me now declare to you,
At something else she'll beat him too.

Let none the Yorkshire girls despise,
Who are so active now a days;
So brisk and nimble they do grow;
That few can match them, I do know;
Then let us stand up for York-shire,
Those country girls I love most dear.

A Yorkshire girl who can outvie
No city girls can them come nigh;
They've rosy blushes in their cheeks,
While city girls are green as leeks;
This with my fancy will agree,
A Yorkshire girl shall be for me.

Then here's a health to a Yorkshire girl,
For in mine eye she is a pearl,
Whose beauty doth so charm mine eye,
That for her I would freely dye;
Her virtues do her face adorn,
And makes her look as fresh as the morn.

Now to conclude, unto my friend
These lines I freely recommend,
Advising him above the rest,
To love a Yorkshire girl the best;
But let him use his skill, for I
Will love a Yorkshire girl until I dye.

THE TWEA THRESHERS

A story of two rustics and the history of their several mistakes during a holiday which they took in 1842 to go to Scarboro' to see the Florentine Venus, then being exhibited in that town.

'Twas on a fiahne cleer sunny day,
Aboot the end 'o summer,
When all the goa was Scarbro' spo,
Between the Tees an Hummer.

Coaches grained 'neath top heavy Leeads,
Gigs, carriages an sike like,
Skew'd dust like fun fra' all the roads,
At' end at Scarbar' tonpike.

Lauk! What a dust there was kick'd up,
Like deed what blustrin storance,
A waint queer seeght was seen that da,
Some waxwark thing fra Florence.

Jerry an Jack, twea threshers bold,
Wer bangin 'oot and barley,
A dusty trade, hard by the road,
Sweeatin' and broilin' rarly.

Dod dang, says Jack, yau knocks and delves,
Digs, plews, sows, maws, an what for?
Pately at yau may live yau's sens,
Bud mare to keep up that, Jer.

He pointed ti twea carriage lead
O' fashionable people;
Wea seem'd to knoo the arts o' ease,
Sat couple feeacing couple.

Why can't we hev a bit o' spree
As weel as uther folks, Jer?
I deean't see why, quoth jer, dang me!
If ahle ageean strike strooak, ser.

Afoor I've seen that Florence thing,
It nobbut costs a shillin';
Beisides I lang ti hev a spree,
An get a thorough swillin'.

Bonni! says Jack, bonni, mi lad,
I like the risolution;
Let's hev thi hand, thi scheeam's weel plan'd,
We'll het i' execution.

Seea Jack and Jer shack'd hands and show'd
'At peasant cud wi peasant,
Like prince wi prince, an' lord wi lord,
Laugh loud, feel pleased, luke pleasant.

Seea yam tha went, wesh'd, scrub'd, and
brush'd,
An' sware tha wad hev rare spooat;
An' eeach put on his bran' new suit,
New breeches, cooat, and waistcooat.

An' off tha went: God speed ya weel!
Cried Jinny, that was Jack's wife;
An' i yer harts his love reveeal,
Cried Fan, the soul o' Jer's life.

I wop yoo'll hev a pleasant da;
I wop yoo will, said Jenny:
I wop we sal, said Jack, hurra!
I wop we sal, said Jerry.

An' tha wer gone, lauk hoo tha preached,
An' laugh'd all't way tha though:
Far on afoor their voices reach'd,
Their mirth was getin' vent so.

The wavy fiels o' yellow wheat,
Spread wide I view ther treasure;
The side swung wots, an' bearded John,
'At fills the tankard measure.

Did sweetly vie wi promises
Zi fill oor barns wi plenty:
Thank God, says Jack, these are his gifts,
Ye fields 'twas him 'at sent ye.

Plenty throned like an empress sat
Upon the broo o' Cayton;
Wea laughed an' made the hills ti smile
For miles round bonny Ayton.

THE YORKSHIRE TIKE

Ah iz' truth a country youth,
Neean us'd teea Lunnon fashions,
Yet vartue guides, an still presides,
Ower all mah steps an' passions.

Neea courtly leear, but all sincere,
Neea bribe shall ivver blinnd me;
If thoo can like a Yorkshire tike,
A rooague tho'll nivver finnd me.

Thof envy's tung, seea slimlee hung,
Wad lee aboot oor country,
Neea men o' t'eearth booast greter wurth,
Or mare extend ther boounty.

Oor northern breeze wi' uz agrees,
An' does for wark weel fit uz;
I' public care, an' all affairs,
Wi honour we acquit uz.

Seea gret a maund is ne'er confiand,
Tiv onny shire or nation;
They geean meeast praise weea weel displays
A leearned iddicasion.

Whahl rancour rolls i' lahtle souls,
By shallo views dissarning,
They're nobbut wise 'at owlus prize
Gud manners, sense and leearnin.

"I don't mind the dust now. My 'DAISY' sucks it all up in a very few minutes!"

Fer 15 guineas I could 'ave 'ad a fotnit i' Scarbro'

MOTORS going at all fast are bound to throw up a great amount of dust. Their speed gives this dust an impetus which flings it often in thick clouds through open windows. Even when not visible, a host of finer particles float through every crevice, and are the despair of the house wife who relies upon sweeping and dusting to keep the home clean. The way out of the difficulty is to use a

"DAISY" Vacuum Cleaner

With the electrically-driven machine illustrated one maid can do single-handed all the cleaning desired.

The Model C. Domestic Machine (electric) costs **15 Guineas.**

For smaller requirements we make manual machines at prices from 42/-

Obtainable of all Ironmongers and Stores.

Write for copy of our Illustrated Booklet "WHO SAID DUST?" Issue No. 8.
It tells all about The "Daisy" Vacuum Cleaner. Address—

THE DAISY VACUUM CLEANER CO., LTD.
GRAVELLY HILL, BIRMINGHAM.

Telephone: 455 & 456 East.
Code—A.B.C. 5th Ed.
AUSTRALASIAN AGENCIES: Rialto, Collins Street, MELBOURNE. 65, Pitt Street, Sydney, N.S.W. Kithers Buildings, King William Street, Adelaide, SOUTH AUSTRALIA. NEW ZEALAND: Strand Arcade, Auckland.

Place-Names

Organic, elemental and highly personal – nothing speaks more eloquently of past lives than place-names. Altered and corrupted over time, they nonetheless hold in perpetuity the sense of home and place that first caused our pioneering ancestors to put down their Yorkshire roots. The homesteads of the ancient Brigante and Parisi tribes have long since disappeared, but vestiges of their place-names remain. Invaders and colonisers – Celts, Romans, Angles, Saxons, Vikings and Normans have also left their marks. Consider this. There is not one anonymous yard in the 3,889,432 acres (more acres than the Bible has words) within the old boundaries of Yorkshire. Every field, every hamlet and hollow, every hill, every crag, every cliff and creek and every watercourse has a name. And what names! Soldiers Lump, Slack, Kettlesing, Boot of the Wold, Lost John's Cave, Land of Nod, Booze, Elysium, Boggarts Roaring Hole, Jump, Wine Haven, The Whams, Great Cockup, Hades, Clint, Shivering Moss, Land of Green Ginger, Hawkswick Chowder, Black Beck Swang, Fill Belly Flat, Greedy Gut and The Tongue.

In Yorkshire, Anglo-Saxon and Danish place-names predominate. Celtic names survive in the nomenclature of rivers, mountains and valleys, whilst Roman names are still attached to the sites of ancient roads and camps. These are just a few simple pointers to the origins of the more common place-names. Those ending in *ton* and *ley* generally indicate an Anglo Saxon (Old English) origin, as do the following: *bury*, *croft*, *den*, *field*, *ford*, *force* or *foss*, *grove*, *ham*, *holt*, *hurst*, and *royd*. Those ending in *by* and *thorpe* frequently indicate a Scandinavian origin, as do the following: *beck*, *fell*, *garth*, *gill*, *holme*, *howe*, *lund*, *ness*, *scar*, *tarn*, *thwaite*, *toft* and *wath*.

Here are just a few place-names and their meanings:

The Old North Riding of Yorkshire

Appletreewick: settlement by the apple trees.
Caldbergh: cold hill.
Clifford: ford by the cliff.

Collingham:	homestead of Col's or Cola's people.
Copmanthorpe:	farmstead or hamlet of the pedlars or chapmen.
Giggleswick:	this is not a summer retreat for Doddy and his Diddymen. The meaning is prosaic indeed: 'the village of Gigel'.

Fryup (Great and Little):
there were no transport cafes or cholestrol girding breakfasts around when these communities were named; their names derive from a combination of the word Freya (a Norse goddess) and *hop* 'enclosed valley'.

Horsehouse: probably the most obviously named village in the whole of Yorkshire, this tiny place in Coverdale takes its name from the equestrian facilities that it provided in abundance during the coaching era. Amazingly, the village once served the main coach route between London and Richmond.

Ingleton:	beacon town or settlement near the peak.
Keld:	spring or well.
Low Bentham:	homestead with bent or coarse grass.
Langstrothdale:	valley of marshy land overgrown with long brushwood.
Markington:	settlement of the Mercians or the land by the boundary.
Newton Kyme:	new settlement of the Kimbe family.
Otley:	Otta's clearing.
Pateley Bridge:	woodland clearing by path.
Ryther:	the cattle island.
Sawley:	hill with willow trees.
Scriven:	place with pits.
Skipton:	sheep farm.
Stalling Busk:	(the) stallion's bush.
Starbotton:	valley where stakes are got.
Tadcaster:	Tada's camp or fortification.
Tockwith:	Toki's wood.
Towton:	Tofi's settlement.
Ugglebarnby:	settlement of Uglubarthr.
Ulleskelf:	Ulfr's bank or hillside.

The Old West Riding of Yorkshire

Baildon: probably, round hill.

Batley: woodland clearing of Bata.

Castleford: ford by the Roman fort.

Clayton West: settlement on clayey soil.

Crofton: farmstead with a croft.

Darfield: open land frequented by deer.

Delph: quarry.

Doncaster: Roman fort on the river Don.

Drax: place of the ferry or portage.

Horbury: stronghold in the mud.

Ingbirchworth: enclosure with the birch trees.

Luddenden: the valley of the river Ludd.

Marsden: probably, boundary valley.

Menston: settlement associated with Mensa.

Mirfield: pleasant open land or open land where festivities are held.

Monk Fryston: farmstead of the Frisians: 'monk' refers to Selby Abbey.

Mytholmroyd: clearing at the confluence.

Normanton: settlement of the Northmen.

Oakworth: oak tree enclosure.

Ossett: Osla's fold or fold frequented by blackbirds.

Penistone: probably, estate by a hill called Penning.

Sheffield: open land by the river Sheaf.

Thorner: thorn bush ridge.

Pontefract: broken bridge.

Royston: farmstead of Hror or Roarr.

Slaithwaite: woodland clearing.

Sowerby: farmstead on sour land.

Sprotborough: the stronghold of Sprota.

Steeton: probably, settlement with stumps.

Swillington: possibly, enclosure near the pig hill or clearing.

Thurstonland: the land of Thorsteinn.

Tong:	settlement in the fork of the river.
Wath:	ford or crossing.
West Bretton:	farmstead of the Britons.
Whitkirk:	white church.
Wombwell:	Wamba's spring or spring in a hollow.
Woodkirk:	church in woodland.

The Old East Riding of Yorkshire

Anlaby:	Olafr's settlement.
Bishop Burton:	fortified farmstead or settlement by the fort.
Ferriby:	settlement by the ferry.
Fridaythorpe:	Frigedæg's hamlet.
Goodmanham:	homestead of Godmund's people.
Hayton:	hay farmstead or hay enclosure.
Hollym:	homestead near the hollow.
Laxton:	estate associated with Leaxa.
Lockington:	estate associated with Loca or fold estate.
Mappleton:	farmstead by the maple tree(s).
Preston:	farmstead of the priests.
Roos:	moor, heath.
Sigglesthorne:	Sigulfr's thorn tree.
Skirlaugh:	bright woodland clearing.
Snaith:	piece of land cut off.
Sproatley:	woodland clearing where shoots grow.
Swine:	channel, creek.
Swinefleet:	swine stream.
Thwing:	narrow strip of land.
Warter:	gallows.
Wetwang:	possibly, place for the trial of a legal action.
Withernwick:	possibly, outlying farm of the place near the thorn tree.
Wharram Percy:	(place at) the kettles or cauldrons (possibly in a topographical sense) (belonging to the) Percy family.

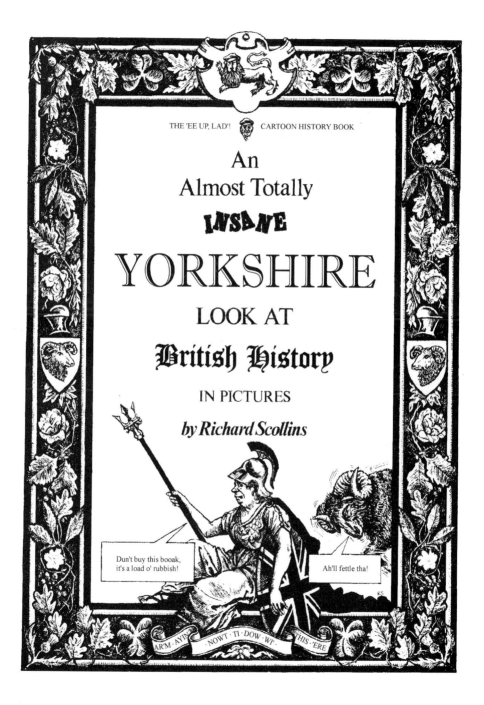

THE 'EE UP, LAD'! CARTOON HISTORY BOOK

An
Almost Totally
INSANE
YORKSHIRE
LOOK AT
British History
IN PICTURES
by Richard Scollins

Dun't buy this booak, it's a load o' rubbish!

Ah'll fettle tha!

AR'M ·AYIN· NOWT ·TI ·DOW ·WI· THIS ·'ERE

Alfred and the Cakes — AD 878

Lady Godiva — AD 1057

The Battle of Hastings — AD 1066

King John and Magna Carta — 1215

The Battle of Agincourt — 1415

Richard III at Bosworth — 1485

Henry VIII and Anne Boleyn — 1529

Raleigh and the Puddle — 1581

Francis Drake Goes Bowling — 1588

The First Night of 'Hamlet' — 1601

The Gunpowder Plot — 1605

The Execution of Charles I — 1649

Charles II and Friends Hide From
the Roundheads — 1651

Isaac Newton Discovers Gravity — 1666

**Bonnie Prince Charlie Arrives
in Scotland — 1745**

Nelson at Trafalgar — 1805

Wellington Inspects His Troops — 1815

The Charge of the Light Brigade — 1854

Stanley Greets Dr. Livingstone — 1871

Queen Victoria 'Not Amused' — 1878

TH'END.